THE FERTILE RHYTHMS

CONTEMPORARY WOMEN

POETS OF MEXICO

THE FERTILE RHYTHMS: CONTEMPORARY WOMEN POETS OF MEXICO

SELECTED AND EDITED BY

THOMAS HOEKSEMA

TRANSLATED BY

THOMAS HOEKSEMA

AND

ROMELIA ENRIQUEZ

LATIN AMERICAN LITERARY REVIEW PRESS
SERIES: DISCOVERIES
PITTSBURGH, PENNSYLVANIA

YVETTE E. MILLER, EDITOR
1989

The Latin American Literary Review Press publishes Latin American creative writing under the series title *Discoveries*, and critical works under the series title *Explorations*.

Library of Congress Cataloging-in-Publication Data

The Fertile rhythms.

(Discoveries)
English and Spanish.
1. Mexican poetry--Women authors. 2. Mexican poetry--20th century. 3. Mexican poetry--Translations into English.
4. English poetry--Translations from Spanish.
I. Hoeksema, Thomas. II. Enríquez, Romelia. III. Series.
PQ7253.F4   1989   861   89-13659
ISBN 0-935480-44-7

This project is supported in part by grants from the National Endowment for the Arts in Washington, D.C., a federal agency, the Arts and Sciences Research Center, New Mexico State University and the Center for Latin American Studies, New Mexico State University.

Graphic designer: James Cardell

Cover photo by Lois Siegel: "The Immortal"

The Fertile Rhythms: Contemporary Women Poets of Mexico may be ordered directly from the publisher:

Latin American Literary Review Press
2300 Palmer Street
Pittsburgh, PA 15218
Tel (412) 351-1477 Fax (412) 351-6831

TABLE OF CONTENTS

Some of the translations included in this volume have appeared in the following journals:

El Ojito
International Poetry Review
Latin American Literary Review
Mid-American Review
Sonora Review
Paintbrush
River Styx
Jacaranda Review
Sulfur
Feminist Studies

NEWS FROM THE FOREST

Gabriel Zaid

The youngest poet in an anthology is in a singular position: at any point of decision he or she could be excluded or recognized finally as worthy of consideration. At times there is consensus: one name is consecrated (almost in a professional way) as "the young poet." In the 1950s the young poet in Mexico was Marco Antonio Montes de Oca, born in 1932. In the 1960s it was Homero Aridjis, born in 1940. In the 1970s no one was so designated. A multitude of poets was born in the 1950s, but no single one was anointed as the latest offspring of the Mexican poetic dynasty.

Some stated that the golden age, initiated at the close of the 19th century, was coming to an end and that it was being sustained only by the great living poets, not by the new generations. The future, they said, was in the novel, a genre that was attracting world attention to Spanish-American writing. No one knows how golden ages begin or end. The great medieval, renaissance, and baroque literary traditions culminated in the mediocrity of the 19th century. Yet, from that mediocrity was born, unexpectedly, a vigorous tradition that continues to the present. There is no assurance that Mexican poetry will maintain its creativity, but it continues today at the level of its most productive epochs.

In 1971, I published *Omnibus de poesía mexicana*. This anthology ranges from indigenous and folk poetry to the most refined, from the 16th to the 20th century. That compilation gave me confidence in the immediate future of poetry in Mexico, and made me feel responsible for understanding what was evolving. Was there anyone to sustain the permanent revitalization initiated by the young Manuel Gutiérrez Nájera (1859-1895)? In 1974, assuming that the problem was cartographic (what was needed were maps of the *terra incognita*), I set to work on an anthology of the most recent poetry.

I soon discovered that it was not possible to accomplish this task in traditional terms. Despite what was being said, talent had not disappeared. On the contrary, it was so abundant that it confounded the expectations of those who wished to isolate a single young poet as the latest successor to the dynasty. There was a profusion of young poets: the dynastic succession was experiencing a population explosion. To do it justice, the traditional anthology was an inadequate form.

Finally, in 1980 I published *Asamblea de poetas jóvenes de México* (siglo xxi, Mexico City) with 164 poets born between 1950 and 1962. To establish a consistent criterion, I read all they had published and did not exclude poets but rather poems, limiting my selection to one poem that I deemed the best in each case. With this criterion, the quality of the group refuted the pessimists. The "Assembly" did justice to the forest if not to the trees.

Ten years later, I am still unable to reduce the plenitude to a few names. Although it is clear that the majority of poets featured in *Asamblea* stopped writing or produced little of note, those who continued growing are still numerous. The forest conceals the trees. For that reason, some recently published traditional selections remain flawed. They are too extensive and yet incomplete. They exclude poets who are equal in quality to those they include. These selections are neither anthologies nor assemblies.

When Thomas Hoeksema proposed translating *Asamblea*, reducing the number of poets and including more than one poem per poet, I was skeptical about the project. I could not see how a coherent subgroup would be determined. Fortunately, an imaginative solution occurred to him: to make a selection of women poets, a project whose final results prove him right. Although he limits himself to the women poets, they represent a good cross-section of the entire generation.

Mexican women have written poetry since the 16th century. The Lady of Tula, concubine of the poet-king Nezahualpilli (son of the poet-king Nezahualcóyotl), "was so wise that she competed with the king and with the wisest in his kingdom; and was in poetry most excellent." The princess Macuilxochitzin (born around 1435) celebrates the conquest of the Aztec empire in 1476:

Like our songs,
Like our flowers,
so, you, the warrior with shaven head
give joy to the Giver of life.

Sor Juana Inés de la Cruz (1651-1695) was so learned that she competed with the most knowledgeable from New Spain and was the preeminent poet in the Hispanic world. Still today, the best poetry written in Mexico equals but does not surpass her poems.

There are a dozen other women writers noted in the centuries of the Vice-Royalty (16th to 18th century) and a hundred or so from the 19th century. Almost all are forgotten. The quality improved in the 20th century with Concha Urquiza (1910-1945) and the generation born between 1917 and 1928 (Margarita Michelena, Emma Godoy, Griselda Alvarez, Guadalupe Amor, Dolores Castro, Margarita Paz Paredes, Rosario Castellanos, Enriqueta Ochoa). They demanded much of themselves and transformed the received poetic language and their own role in the world of culture. Almost all began with a Catholic, literary, feminine militancy patterned after Sor Juana or Gabriela Mistral (A frequent visitor to Mexico who won the Nobel Prize for literature in 1945). They aspired to professional status and to be recognized through their work, not to be seen merely as daughters or wives who wrote. The nun and women who teach were their emancipated models.

The example spread. Two generations later, one-fifth of the poets in *Asamblea* are women, a proportion never seen before in Mexican poetry. But the greatest change is qualitative. If one compares the two anthologies published to celebrate the 4th centennial of the discovery of America (*Poetisas mexicanas*, 1893 by José María Vigil and *Antología de poetas mexicanos*, 1894 from the Academy), it is obvious that the women in these collections focus on family life and write at an inferior level. In contrast, the women of *Asamblea* cannot be distinquished from the men poets, either in quality or in professional activities.

The *Asamblea* group reflects a university generation that has studied literature (primarily), arts, humanities, and, in some cases, (curiously enough) economics. Their adolescence and early youth coincide with the peak of the Mexican economy, a situation quite conducive to cultural development (until the crisis that began in 1982). Like no other generation, this group had opportunities for study, travel, grants, publication, jobs, and supplemental income from cultural activities.

Another distinguishing point is that this group publishes its own literary journals, however ephemeral, and in surprising numbers (nearly 50 appeared and disappeared between 1976 and 1979). The previous generation did not exhibit such editorial fervor, nor is it repeated in the succeeding one. Paradoxically, the *Asamblea* group writes little: the total number of poems published is relatively low, and the prose production either does not exist or is very slight. Of note is their interest in the poetry of other languages (especially English and French), which they read and translate.

In all this, there are no major differences between men and women, not even in the themes or stylistic preferences. Perhaps there is in the women's poetry a greater disregard of epigrammatical forms, a marked preference for the mysterious or less obvious poetry, and subjects and themes more centered in the sentient or corporal "I" than in the historical or reflective "I." But these are features common to the whole generation, the first one that seems to be intellectually unisex.

It is unusual for the younger generation to make poetry newer. In recent years, the most radically new poetry written in Mexico is found in *Picos pardos* (1986), a book written by Gerardo Deniz at age 52. Typically, young poetry exhibits sensibility, talent, and craft without producing *un frisson nouveau*. There are illustrious examples to the contrary: Ramón López Velarde (1888-1921) and Carlos Pellicer (1897-1977) wrote a radically new poetry before age 33. But virtually all the great Mexican poets have written their most innovative poetry after their youthful period.

From among the women of the *Asamblea* group have emerged vigorous literary personalities that in some cases overflow from poetry to the theater, the novel, criticism, and journalism. There is even the seed of a radically new poetry in Coral Bracho. But writing poetry cannot be reduced to making history, nor can it be judged solely from this point of view. If this generation has not yet made history, it has certainly created a poetry that confirms the generous sap of the forest that attracts through its richness, its mystery, and its introspective vitality— those fertile rhythms to which Thomas Hoeksema has responded.

FOREWORD

The Fertile Rhythms: Contemporary Women Poets of Mexico, we are told in the introduction by Gabriel Zaid, is an anthology of poems which represents the new generation of Mexican poets and yet were all written by women poets—is not that a miracle? Is it possible that, in Mexico at any rate, the woman poet is no longer an anomaly as she was called by Joanna Bankier, co-editor of *Woman Poets of the World* in her 1984 preface to my anthology, *Woman Who Has Sprouted Wings: Poems By Contemporary Latin American Women Poets*? Only five years have passed since my book first appeared, yet it appears that a new generation of women poets, born between 1950-1962, has begun writing in Mexico under entirely new conditions, for, according to Zaid, the women poets represented in *The Fertile Rhythms* not only write like men but have credentials that equal those of male poets.

No doubt readers will have many questions to ask: How can poems by women represent a generation? Don't women's poems still concentrate on the traditional women's themes of religion, love, marriage, home, and children that male readers have found so uninteresting? How can women's poems lay claim to universality? What kind of emotional stance do these poems by women take before the world? Are they only vehicles for women's anger at society?

In several ways, then, these poems will not conform to the reader's expectations: instead of the expected women's tone of anger or earnestness, they are marked by a distancing from emotion, a kind of coolness and irony; instead of the usual women's themes, these poems often do not present a subject in the accepted sense; instead of an identification of woman with the earth, they seem to exist in space, without location in a real physical world. These poems do not reflect the tradition of

Mexican women's poetry established by Sor Juana and carried on by Rosario Castellanos. In many respects, these poems belong more to the world than to Mexico.

What most distinguishes this anthology of poems by a new generation of Mexican poets, all of them women born between 1950 and 1962, is a love of language:

> At times the angels prefer dark words,
> all bloodied and angular, they moan: like mercury fish
> strung together.

(Hilda Bautista)

Their poetry is the outpouring, the flood, of language by which they define themselves, the world, and poetry itself. Not events, but language seems to be regarded as the source of experience. The language here (or languages) is exuberant, assertive and self-assured, daring, confident, at times experimental:

> (Wrapped in the evening breeze, the violet sound
> purified, the child, with the velvet base of his probing
> tongue, touches,
> from that smooth, indefensible lust—sensitive iris that
> submits to the rocks
> if it foresees the stigma,
> the scorching light—the substance, the pure
> and vibrant tuft—on its relaxed, absorbed petal—
> (half-opened
> gem that quivers; udders), soothing acidic juice,
> the marsh, (ice), the lambent sap (cabala),
> nectar of the firefly).

(Coral Bracho)

Often these poems seem to belong to what, in this country, is called "language poetry," a poetry whose prime consideration is language and the qualities of language rather than ideas or subject matter or even considerations of form. As a result, sometimes it is difficult to determine what a specific poem is "about," or how it relates to what we call "reality." Are these poems "mapping consciousness"? Are they attempts to discover a new self through language explorations?

15

Sometimes they seem to be:

> Fragments flee
> Stifling my architecture   with blows
> (unfinished act   a futile form)
> Sleepwalking artists
> Create absences in the framework of my heart
> The night soars on schedule
> Pain curves without epicenter
> Above my perfect back.

(Adriana Yáñez)

Many of these poems are delivered in a tone of irony, a philosophical and distanced irony in which subjectivity is replaced by a stance of objectivity:

> everything immobile becomes more real
> foliage is the fermented calm of the air
> your movement the leaves
> I'm not surprised if day by day
> strength merges with the body
> strength that appears when death draws near

(Lilia Barbachano)

In fact, irony seems to express their most constant attitude toward the world they confront. One poem by Socorro León Femat begins:

> But the door that faces the void
> is open day and night

And ends:

> With an abnormal loneliness that leads us astray
> we walk like tormented prey
> searching in every section
> of the house in the city in a face
> that resembles ourselves.

(Socorro León Femat)

Sometimes the irony deepens into sarcasm:

> The good people reverse
> the meaning of words
> and live their life like a flowing spring.
>
> All of them go to heaven in a band
> without thought   conflict
> contradiction or madness.

(Socorro León Femat)

But the sarcasm can be light-hearted too:

> Recognizing myself as prey
> and convinced there is no greater glory than the
>   offering of a virgin neck to you,
> nor greater goodness than that inscribed in your painful,
>   slow,
>   interminable
>   and lovingly
>   cruel attack

(Carmen Boullosa)

Sometimes the irony turns to despair:

> But the memories waste away
> unable to support their excessive reality.
> It happens that memory also grows weary.
> It happens that memory chooses to immerse itself
> in the lethargy of silence.

(Perla Schwartz)

Or again:

> And here I am
>
> in this landscape of ashes.

(Blanca Luz Pulido)

Mostly, in this collection of poems, women's traditional themes are absent—religion, love, marriage, children, the domestic life—or they appear with a difference, as in "Ideological Contradictions on Washing a Plate." Does this mean that the gap between what interests women and what interests men has narrowed? Do traditional women's lives bore women? Certainly the ordinary, daily events of household routine do not appear here with any frequency. On the other hand, neither do the great "universal" themes of war, politics, and world history. Even the theme of feminist protest does not appear. Indeed, in a number of poems subject has become secondary to language. When these poems do exhibit identifiable themes, they may be about identity, time, language, sex, death, and fear.

Moreover, the personal "I" so often noted as typical of contemporary women's poetry in this hemisphere is absent. Another "I" appears in its place: androgynous, self-confident, playful. Sometimes this "I" defends tradition—wearing makeup, for example.

I put on eye make-up
not as a stupid automatism
but because it is the only moment in the day

when I return to the times of other people and

my hand changes to an Egyptian hand and

the dash on the eye remains in History.

(Kyra Galván)

Sometimes the "I" makes love, and when the narrator speaks of love, the reader usually cannot tell whether the love subject is male or female, whether the love is erotic or platonic. This is especially surprising when one considers that these women poets are between 27-39 years old, in the very time of life when the reader might expect them to be writing about their love affairs, marriage, and children. When she does appear, the woman lover, the "I," speaks with self-confidence, even aggressiveness:

The two men I love are vicious
but adorable
I have sent flowers to their cabin
as well as good and bad verses,
it seems that I play the gentleman

(Vera Larrosa)

Not infrequently the poems are impersonal, and the "I" is philosophical and reflective:

> Because I reflect
> in pauses
> and silence
> that lead
> nowhere
> because I am
> of shadow,
> because I do not engage
> the whiteness
> of the hours.

(Laura González Durán)

Generally, the "I" doesn't seem to have considered women's traditional diffidence as a possible role; the speaker seems to have assumed an assertiveness that comes naturally:

> I will tell you: I am cedar woman agony woman
>   woman like a wheatfield   like a violet
>   like a watermelon and a storm.
> I seek an island for gestation,
> to fashion my liberty and my body
>   and all my movements.

(Kyra Galván)

The identification of woman with nature in these lines by Kyra Galván (which echo the endless poem of Maria Sabina, a Mexican Native American woman poet) is not typical of the poems in this collection; mostly, women's identification with nature is absent in these poems. There is no Earth Goddess here. No earth mother with full breasts and thighs though the poet may identify herself with the universe. Indeed, in one poem, the male seems to be the Earth:

> I drink (your exposed, permeable roots;
> on your wanton shores
> —seething mire—moors) the mossy designs, your
> thick sap (mound of drunken vines) I smell
> in your deep vigilant borders, embers,
> cascades within your oily jungles. I hear
> (your tactile semen) the lodes, larvae (fertile apse) I feel
> in your living marshes, your mud: trails,

in your embracing forge: the clues

(Coral Bracho)

Additionally, the sense of place in these poems is not rooted in physical location as the Earth:

I write to you from the landscapes
still unknown to me,
from evenings I recall
although I was never there.
I write to you from the night,
from the darkness that
mysteriously invades the corners
of the tiny house
where I still do not live.

(Laura González Durán)

The speakers in these poems rove through the universe, very much at home and very much in command:

You have risen to the light of my two eyes,
my blood enriches you,
and my veins exalt you.

Without knowing it you move closer to your form,
and you will kindle the flame
in the endless night that awaits you.

Without knowing it you will write your name,
your unborn name, between my lips.

(Blanca Luz Pulido)

When these women poets do speak of love, they seem either to assume equality:

our passion is born of two;
arithmetical heart with
a solid trapeze base.

(Perla Schwartz)

Or associating it with anger, they see the anger as the means to something new:

> Love, with rage
> split the rock for me
> with all your animal desperation
> until sparks ignite;
> the indivisible hurts me more than what is broken
> with rage, love, with rage
>
> (Sabina Berman)

These poems, as Anäis Nin says poems should, "help us to see more, to hear more, to discover within ourselves" what we had only previously guessed was there. Does this mean that a new generation of Mexican women poets is creating a new life, a new language, a new power for women? Perhaps it is the lengthy tradition that women poets have enjoyed in Mexico going back at least to the Aztecs and in historical times to the great Sor Juana that has made all the difference. After all, these young women poets have immediately behind them a great generation of women poets that includes, among others, Rosario Castellanos, Ulalume González de León, Isabel Fraire, Thelma Nava, and they live in a country in which poetry is so important that you can buy it everywhere, even in the airports.

Mostly, the female identity that these women poets seek or see or define is not the traditional, passive, nurturing identity, but one that acknowledges the right of a woman to her own needs and to the nurturing of her needs. We can only congratulate them, wonder at their assertiveness and self-confidence, and hope with them to see every woman "enter her interior":

> After a few moments of fixing her hair,
> she understands it is time to prepare the hooks
> and like those men that probe the sea
> to enter her interior and fish for herself.
>
> (Hilda Bautista)

MARY CROW
Colorado State University
Fort Collins, Colorado

The Fertile Rhythms

PATRICIA ALVAREZ AVENDAÑO

La Historia Coincidió

La historia coincidió
con el suicidio de las telas traslúcidas
las torres altas
y los trigos amplios,
todo tenía algo de locura tierna,
de manchas de colores
mientras los espejos transformaban los sepias
con cielos en peligro de vientos del norte.
Hasta entonces el otoño
había quedado solitario.

PATRICIA ALVAREZ AVENDAÑO

History Coincided

History coincided
with the suicide of translucent webs
soaring towers
and spacious fields of wheat,
everything possessed a bit of tender madness,
of stains and colors
while mirrors altered the sepias
with skies menaced by north winds.
Until then autumn
had endured alone.

LILIA BARBACHANO

Mi Tiempo

ese rodearse de murallas de pozos de peces
ese hundirse en la tarea de ir midiendo
día a día las cucharadas
habitadas por las horas
cuerpos con olor a cuerpos
causalidad del instante
sólo quedan los dedos quemados
en el incendio de los naipes
plausible la inmovilidad del tedio
así papel o invento
olor a lo que es sueño a boca del sueño
inmensidad dulce y pastosa

en la mano se ha desvanecido una estela
no quedan las huellas en lo que fluye
se van las huellas
y todo inmóvil es más real
es la calma lúdica del aire el follaje
tu agitación las hojas
no me asombro si día a día
la fuerza incorpora el cuerpo
esa fuerza de cuando se a acerca el tiempo de morir

LILIA BARBACHANO

My Time

surrounding myself with walls and tanks of fish
submerging myself in the task of measuring
each day the spoonfuls
inhabited by the hours
bodies with the smell of bodies
causality of the moment
only scorched fingers remain
in the fire of the cards
the admirable immobility of boredom
thus paper or invention
the odor of what is dream at the dream's mouth
a sweet and pasty expanse

in the hand a trail has vanished
no traces remain in the flow
the traces disappear
everything immobile becomes more real
foliage is the fermented calm of the air
your movement the leaves
I'm not surprised if day by day
strength merges with the body
strength that appears when death draws near

LILIA BARBACHANO

Aldebarán

a la memoria de Howard Phillips Lovecraft

Perderse por Alejandría
ligera como las medusas
libre ya de las ataduras
de mi sombra encadenada.

Aldebarán al desprenderse
en transparente libélula
se introduce en el mediodía
caliente y profundo del huerto.

Su presencia invade mi mente
como un sueño detrás de un sueño
verde espejo de crisálidas
limite entre los litorales.

Siento su lenqua marfilina
bosque intranquilo de caoba y sal
cuando lame oculta mis labios
sin nunca llegar a conocerme.

En los confines del pensamiento
pretendo detenerlo en fuego
desvanecerlo en blanco eléboro
romperlo en suave aliento.

LILIA BARBACHANO

Aldebarán

in memory of Howard Phillips Lovecraft

Losing himself via Alexandria
nimble as a jellyfish
already free from the tethers
of my chained shadow.

Aldebarán releases himself
in a transparent dragonfly
and penetrates the warm and
deepening noon of the orchard.

His presence invades my mind
like a dream behind a dream
a green mirror of chrysalises
boundary between seacoasts.

I feel his ivory tongue
restless forest of mahogany and salt
when he licks he conceals my lips
never really knowing me.

On the edges of thought
I try to seal him in fire
reducing him to white hellebores
breaking him with gentle breaths.

HILDA BAUTISTA

A veces los ángeles prefieren las palabras negras,
gimen sangrientos, angulares; como ensartados peces de
mercurio.
Son las sombras equívocas del verbo.
Sus imágenes rotas yacen turbias bajo frenéticos pozos de
arcilla.
Reptan, chocan sus vientres imperfectos,
sus hediondas espadas de fundido hierro.
Parciales, soplan.
En el viento son olas de juguete,
angustiosos momentos encrespados por los que el tiempo pesa.
Quizá el pronunciamiento pertenece al llamativo cinto,
el secreto del infimo universo inexplicado.
Pero ellos, tersos y otoñales,
brillan en vuelo fascinante; sol de soles.
Son casi la mentira suficiente
partida en los espejos fragmentados que se pintan de luz en la
marea.

HILDA BAUTISTA

At times the angels prefer dark words,
all bloodied and angular, they moan; like mercury fish strung
together.
They are the ambiguous shadows of the word.
Their broken images lay muddied under furious pools of clay.
They crawl, startling their imperfect bellies,
their smelly swords of fused iron.
Incomplete, they gasp.
They are waves of toys in the wind,
anquished moments angered by those that time oppresses.
Perhaps the pronouncement belongs to the gaudy belt,
the secret of the wretched unexplained universe.
But they, smooth and autumnal,
shine in fascinating flight; sun of suns.
They are almost the suitable lie
scattered in the fragments of mirror that paint themselves with
light on the tide.

HILDA BAUTISTA

Una mujer se asoma temprano a la ventana,
mientras mira los muelles va soltando la ropa.
Camina lentamente hasta quedar desnuda
y respira el olor agradable de invierno.
De pronto se descubre adentro del espejo.
Ese reflejo helado es más fiel que ella misma.
No es nuevo pero muestra una parte del alma
que sólo encuentra al verse caminando desnuda.
Regresa a la ventana cuando los pescadores
se suben a sus barcas con las cañas al hombro
y la neblina cede para que el puerto se abra.
Después de unos minutos en que se arregla el pelo,
comprende que es el tiempo de tomar los anzuelos
y como aquellos hombres que buscan en el mar
entrar en su interior a pescarse a sí misma.

HILDA BAUTISTA

A woman leans out of the window at dawn,
removes her clothes while staring at the docks.
She walks slowly until naked
and breathes the satisfying smell of winter.
Suddenly she finds herself inside the mirror.
A cold reflection more faithful than she herself,
It's not new but reveals a part of the soul
she encounters only when walking naked.
She returns to the window when the fishermen
enter their boats carrying fishing poles on their shoulders
and the fog recedes so the port is opened.
After a few moments of fixing her hair,
she understands it is time to prepare the hooks
and like those men that probe the sea
to enter her interior and fish for herself.

SABINA BERMAN

Rojo

Ayer, cuando el deseo
se nos desató en pasión,
rasguñé tu hombro,
y luego, bajo el árbol estremecido
de tus sollozos,
besé la herida

¿Cómo explicarás la marca
a tus otras amantes?

Hasta nuestro próximo encuentro
me anhelarás
con un poco de odio

SABINA BERMAN

Red

Yesterday, when desire
released us in passion,
I scratched your shoulder,
and then, under the quivering tree
of your sobs,
I kissed your wound

How will you explain the mark
to your other lovers?

Until our next meeting
your longing for me
will be tinged with hatred

CARMEN BOULLOSA

Carta al Lobo

Querido Lobo:
Llego aquí después de cruzar el mar abierto del bosque,
el mar vegetal que habitas,
el abierto de ira en la oscuridad y en la luz que lo cruza
    a hurtadillas,
en su densa, inhabitable noche de aullidos que impera
    incluso de día o en el silencio,
mar de resmas de hojas
que caen y caen y crecen y brotan, todo al mismo tiempo,
de yerbas entrelazadas,
de mareas de pájaros,
de oleadas de animales ocultos.

Llegué aquí cruzando el puente que une al mundo
    temeroso con tu casa,
este lugar inhóspito,
inhóspito porque está la mar de habitado,
habitado como el mar.

En todo hay traición porque todo está vivo...
Por ejemplo, aquello, si desde aquí parece una sombra,
¿hacia dónde caminará cuando despierte?
Como fiera atacará cuando pase junto a él,
cuando furioso conteste al sonido de mis pasos.
Así todo lo que veo.
En todo hay traición

...era el camino, lobo,
la ruta que me llevaba a ti...

Escucha mi delgada voz, tan cerca.
Ya estoy aquí.

CARMEN BOULLOSA

Letter to the Wolf

Dear Wolf:
I arrive here after crossing the open sea of the forest,
the vegetal sea where you live,
the open space of wrath in the darkness and the light that
      slinks across it,
in its thick, forsaken night of howls that prevails
      enclosed by day or in silence,
sea with reams of leaves
that fall and fall and grow and bud, all at the same time,
of snarled weeds,
tides of birds,
waves of hidden animals.

I arrived here crossing the bridge that connects the timid
      world with your house,
this unfriendly place,
unfriendly because it is the inhabited sea,
inhabited like the sea.

There is treachery in everything because everything is alive...
for example, that, if from here it looks like a shadow,
where will it go when it awakens?
Like a beast it will attack when I come near,
when angry it might respond to the sound of my footsteps.
The same with everything I see.
There is treachery in everything

...it was the road, wolf,
the path that draws me to you...

Listen to my feeble voice, so near.
Now I am here.

Escoge de lo que traje
lo que te plazca.
Casi no puedes mirarlo,
insignificante como es,
perdido en la espesura que habitas.
Estoy aquí para ofrecerte mi cuello,
mi frágil cuello de virgen,
un trozo pálido de carne con poco, muy poco que roerle,
tenlo, tenlo.
¡Apresura tu ataque!
¿Te deleitarás con el banquete?
(No puedo, no tengo hacia dónde escapar
y no sé si al clavarme los dientes
me mirarás a los ojos).

Reconociéndome presa
y convencida de que no hay mayor grandeza que la del cuello
    de virgen entregándose a ti,
ni mayor bondad que aquella inscrita en tu doloroso,
                    lento,
                    interminable
                    y cruel
                    amoroso ataque,
cierro esta carta.
Sinceramente tuya,
                    Carmen

Choose from what I brought
whatever pleases you.
You can barely see it,
insignificant as it is,
lost in the thicket where you live.
I am here to offer you my neck,
my fragile, virginal neck,
a pale morsel of flesh with little, very little to gnaw,
take it, take it.
Hasten your attack!
Will the feast give you pleasure?
(None for me, I am unable to escape
and I wonder if you will look into my eyes
as you sink your fangs).

Recognizing myself as prey
and convinced there is no greater glory than the
                    offering of a virgin neck to you,
nor greater goodness than that inscribed in your painful,
                                        slow,
                                        interminable
                                        and lovingly
                                        cruel attack,
I close this letter.
Sincerely yours,
                    Carmen

CORAL BRACHO

Sobre Las Mesas: El Destello*

> El rizoma, como tallo subterráneo... tiene, en
> sí mismo, muy diversas formas: desde su
> extensión superficial ramificada en todos
> sentidos, hasta su concreción en bulbos y
> tubérculos.
>   El deseo es un creador de realidad... produce
> y se mueve mediante rizomas.
>   Un rasgo intensivo comienza a actuar por su
> cuenta...
>
>   Deleuze y Guattari, *Rizoma*

En la palabra seca, informulada, se estrecha,
rancia membrana parda ((decir: fina gota de aceite
    para el brillo matinal
de los bordes, para la línea
tibia, transitada, que cruza, como un puro matiz, sobre
el vasto crepitar, sobre el lomo colmado,
bulbo —una gota de saliva animal:
para las inflexiones, para el alba fecundada (caricia)
que se expande a la orilla, como una espuma, un
    relieve;
un pelaje frutal— una llaga de luz, un hilván: para
los gestos aromados al tacto, a la sombra rugosa,
    codiciante;
una voz, una fibra desprendida —un vellón— al azar
    de las gubias, del frote plectro),
en la cumbre, al ijar, de las imantaciones;
Tientos

y el idioma capilar de los roces en el cuenco lobular
de los cuerpos. Púrpura
en la raíz;

*Esto es un corte de rizoma visto al microscopio; la perdiz es una
célula de papa. Lo demás aparece o forma parte del paisaje: búsquese
en él lo alusivo a la libido de los caballos.

CORAL BRACHO

On the Facets: The Flashing*

> The rhizome, like a subterranean stalk...
> assumes, by itself, very diverse shapes:
> from its superficial extension magnified in
> many ways, to its manifestation in bulbs and
> tubers.
> Desire is the creator of reality...it produces
> and moves forward by means of rhizomes.
> An intensive feature begins to act by
> itself...
>
> Deleuze and Guattari, *Rhizomes*

In the parched word, unformulated, it shrinks,
rancid brown membrane ((that is: a delicate drop of oil for the
    morning radiance
of the boundaries, for the tepid
line, well-traveled, that crosses, like a limpid hue, above
the vast sizzling, over the burdened back,
bulb —a drop of animal saliva:
for the inflections, for the fertilized dawn (caress)
which expands to the shore, like foam, a
    relief;
a fruit-bearing fur— an ulcer of light, a basting: for
expressions fragrant to the touch, to the wrinkled shadow,
    coveted;
a voice, a loose fiber —a fleece— at random from the chisels,
    from the strum of the pick)
on the crest, at the flank, of the magnetizations;
Strokings

and the hair language of rubbings in the lobed bowl
of the bodies. Purple
at the root;

---

* A rhizome section seen by microscope; the partridge is a potato cell.
The rest appears to be or forms part of the landscape: examine it for
what is connected to the libido of horses.

una esponja, una lima, un espejo
axilar: y en los ecos,

la estatura:
una alondra. Rimas en los espliegos;
hielo: por la grupa liminal, tersos belfos inquietos.
Valva pilosa,
alianza, en el vuelco; plexos y el tendón:
un ardor, una punta sinovial en los goces veteados:
    ductos
a la pálida cima oculta;
una astilla, una cinta (gato),
un embrión para el bronce de espesuras rampantes,
    intimables;
un hervor, una turba despeinada, una espora:

Caudas entornadas al auge de un sabor inguinal.
    Sobre las crines; coces:

En las hormas habituales, impugnadas, de estar, en
sus zagas humosas, ovulantes:
                un carámbano exacto,
                    un candil.
Riscos.

y en los pliegues enlamados, los atisbos de estar,
en sus médanos acres:
higos perlados; risas;

un limón en las orlas incitadas;
rasgar: con almohazas vidriantes, inaudibles (vino
    prensil, hirsuto).
con espinas el temple, las pezuñas;

carcajada chispeante entre los bulbos
escrutados, las urracas;
                fósforos, guiños, ecos
                en la tenaza; salta
                la perdiz.

La perdiz: ave fresca, abundante, de muslos gruesos;
acusado dimorfismo sexual. Sus plumas rojas,
    cenicientas,

a sponge, a lime, an axillary
mirror: and in the echoes,
stature:
a lark. Rhymes in the lavender;
ice: by the liminal rump, smooth restless animal lips.
Hirsute valve,
alliance, in the overturning; plexus and tendon:
a warmth, a synovial point under the veined delights:
    ducts
to the pale hidden summit;
a splinter, a ribbon (cat),
an embryo for the bronze of rampant thickets,
    intimable;
a boiling, a dishevelled mass, a spore:

Cope-tails ajar at the peak of an inguinal taste.
    Above the manes; kicks:

In the customary moulds, challenged, of existing, in
their smoky, ovulating rears:
                a precise icicle,
                    an oil-lamp.

Cliffs.

and in the slimy folds, hints of existing,
and on its pungent banks of sand;
pearly figs; laughter;

a lemon on the excited fringes;
tearing; with inaudible glazed currycombs (wine, prehensile
    and shaggy),
with thorns the mood, the hooves;

sparking laughter between the inspected
bulbs, the magpies;
                phosphorus, winks, echoes
                in the claw; the partridge
                leaps.

The partridge: fresh bird, plentiful, with solid thighs;
marked sexual dimorphism. Its red feathers,
    ashen,

encubren. Salta en parábola eyecta sobre las fresas;
aleteante calidez. Tiene los flancos grises (Las fresas
bullen esponjadas, exhalan —de sus cienos de amapola,
de entresijo verbal— la lejia delectante), las patas
    finas,
el vuelo corto; corre (los sabores suntuosos, apilables)
con rapidez.

        Abre sus belfos limpios:
el jugo moja y perfuma su atelaje; en su piel
de escozores ambiguos, ávido ciñe el grácil,
respingante; lúbrico abisma el néctar
simultáneo; estupor; estupor anchuroso
entre los brotes atiplados;
hincar, en las corvas deslumbrantes, erectas.
En los bíceps, los escrotos; Fúlgidos, agrios. Trotes.
    Alentado a las ancas
alumbradas; cadencias; ritmos convexos; malvos
    paroxismos: de bruces
entre las hondas resonancias. Pedúnculos emprendibles
    bajo el cinto:

Libar desde las formas borboteantes; la lengua entre
    las texturas engranadas, las vulvas
prístinas en sus termas; lluvia a los núcleos
astillados; rizomas incontenibles entre los flujos, las
    pelambres exultadas, espumantes, de estar;
bajo las riendas fermentables, las gualdrapas.
    Embebido
en las blandas, extensivas. Desbordado.
Volúmenes irascibles entre la paja exacerbada,
    germinante. Vital,
inmarcesible en sus impulsos abruptos, suave y
    matizado en sus ocres,
su esplendor, a las yemas; único a las pupilas
restregantes.
Desbandada encendida entre los surcos, las pimientas,
    los indicios; densa
y exaltable en sus puntas: al olfato. Ráfaga
mineral. Un renglón, un cabús, un polvito; Gárgola.
Una hormiga en las crestas hilarantes, por los muslos,
el vientre; en las palabras)) tensas, enturbiadas,
se estrecha, ronca membrana ((cítricas. La estridencia
    perpetrable en los

conceal. Leaps in ejective parabola above the strawberries;
a fluttering fever. Has gray flanks (Boiling
spongy strawberries, they exhale —from their poppy swamps,
from their verbal mesentery— the delectable lye), slender
    legs,
a short flight; it runs (sumptuous, overflowing taste)
rapidly.

        Opens its full clean lips:
the juice moistens and scents its harness; on its skin
of random stings, eagerly encircles the graceful one,
kicking; the slippery simultaneous nectar
sinks; amazement; vast amazement
among the high-pitched buds;
kneeling, on dazzling knee-backs, erect.
On the bicep, the scrotums; Radiant, acrid. Trots.
    Curbed by the illuminated
rumps; cadences; convex rhythm; violet-colored
        paroxysms: face down
among deep resonances. Extendible peduncles
    below the belt:

Sucking from the bubbling shapes; the tongue between
        the linking textures, pristine
vulvas in thermal springs, rain for the splintered
nuclei; turbulent rhizomes between the streams, the
        jubilant, foaming furs of existence;
beneath fermentable reins, the blankets.
    Absorbed
in the beds, expansive. Inundated.
Sensitive forms through the exacerbated straw, sprouting. Vital,
imperishable in their sudden impulses, smooth and tainted
    by their ocher,
their splendor, in their yolks; unique to the rubbing
pupils.
Stampede of flames between the furrow, the peppers, the
    traces; dense
and exaltable on their tips: by smell. Mineral
burst. A line, a caboose, a speck of dust; Gargoyle.
An ant in the joyful tufts, by the thighs,
the belly; in words)) taut, murky,
it shrinks, harsh membrane ((citric. The perpetual
    shrillness on the

lindes)) parda; su red empaña ((en los ápices
lubricados, el pistilo.

—Su voz: saboreando, exhibiendo, despojándolo— Luz;
en los espacios excitables, el acto sedicioso. Labial,
embarnecible bajo el índice fresco, su tersura;
prensan.

Magnetismo atizado hasta el exceso degustable,
el rechinido. Vértices las cosquillas.
—Acedando, exprimiéndolo— en rupturas desbocadas,
expresivas. Vórtice. Entre los fierros, los erizos,
el instinto. Roedores inexpugnables
entre los hilos, las escuadras, el cedazo. Un terrón,
un respiro lanceolado, un prurito.
Rastrean bajo las zonas apiñadas, intensivas.
Nudos papilares entre la yerba. Sobre las mesas: el
destello.
Un punzón, un insecto en las palabras)) lentas, em-
palmadas ((entre las grietas las cesuras, en las bridas.
Súbitos y lascivos las concentran —Su voz: separándolo,
abriéndolo, eligiendo—, ciñen y cohabitan en los filos
espejeantes)), huecas; su costra opaca ((entre los gri-
tos, las cernejas, los resquicios. Estar:))

edges)) drab; its net dims ((on the lubricated boundaries,
the   pistil.

—His voice: savoring, performing, plundering it— Light;
in excitable spaces, the seditious act. Labial,
expandable below the cool forefinger, its smoothness; they
press.

Magnetism aroused to tasty excess,
the grating. The tickling summits.
—Turning sour, squeezing— in wild splittings,
tender. Vortex. Between the irons, the thistles,
instinct. Stubborn rodents
among the threads, the squares, the sieve. A clod,
a lanceolate breath, an itch.
To trail below the jammed, intensive zones.
Papillary knots among the grass. On the facets: the
    flashing.
An awl, an insect in the words)) sluggish,
crammed ((between the cracks the caesuras, on the reins.
Sudden and wanton they focus them— His voice: slitting it,
opening it, choosing it— they encircle and cohabit on reflecting
edges)), hollows; their opaque crust ((among the screams,
the fetlocks, the clefts. To exist:))

CORAL BRACHO

Una Luciérnaga Bajo La Lengua

Te amo desde el sabor inquieto de la fermentación;
en la pulpa festiva. Insectos frescos, azules.
En el zumo reciente, vidriado y dúctil.
Grito que destila la luz:
por las grietas frutales;
bajo el agua musgosa que se adhiere a las sombras. Las papilas,
                                                    las grutas.
En las tintas herbáceas, instilantes, Desde el tacto azorado.
Brillo que rezuma, agridulce: de los goces feraces,
de los juegos hendidos por la palpitación.
                    Gozne
(Envuelto por el aura nocturna, por los ruidos violáceos,
acendrados, el niño, con la base mullida de su lengua expectante,
                                                    toca,
desde esa tersa, insostenible, lubricidad —lirio sensitivo que se
    pliega a las rocas
si presiente el estigma, el ardor de la luz— la sustancia, la arista
vibrante y fina —en su pétalo absorto, distendido— (joya
que palpita entreabierta; ubres), el ácido
zumo blando (hielo), el marisma,
la savia tierna (cábala), el néctar
    de la luciérnaga).

CORAL BRACHO

Firefly Under the Tongue

From the restless taste of fermentation I love you:
in the festive pulp. Fresh blue insects.
Glazed and pliant in the newborn juice.
A scream distilled by light:
through fruitful crevices;
under the mossy water that clings to shadows. Papillas,
                                                    caverns.
In permeating herbaceous hues. From the startled touch.
Radiance that oozes bittersweet: from the fertile pleasures,
of games severed by palpitation.
                    Hinge
(Wrapped in the evening breeze, the violet sound,
purified, the child, with the velvet base of his probing tongue,
                                                    touches,
from that smooth, indefensible lust —sensitive iris that submits
    to the rocks
if it forsees the stigma,
the scorching light—the substance, the pure
and vibrant tuft—on its relaxed, absorbed petal—(half-opened
gem that quivers; udders), soothing acidic juice,
the marsh, (ice), the lambent sap (cabala),
nectar of the firefly).

CORAL BRACHO

Oigo tu cuerpo con la avidez abrevada y tranquila
de quien se impregna (de quien
emerge,
de quien se extiende saturado,
recorrido
de esperma) en la humedad
cifrada (suave oráculo espeso; templo)
en los limos, embalses tibios, deltas,
de su origen; bebo
(tus raíces abiertas y penetrables; en tus costas
lascivas —cieno bullente— landas)
los designios musgosos, tus savias densas
(parva de lianas ebrias) Huelo
en tus bordes profundos, expectantes, las brasas,
en tus selvas untuosas,
las vertientes. Oigo (tu semen táctil) los veneros, las larvas;
(ábside fértil) Toco
en tus ciénegas vivas, en tus lamas: los rastros
   en tu fragua envolvente: los indicios
(Abro
a tus muslos ungidos, rezumantes; escanciados de luz) Oigo
en tus légamos agrios, a tu orilla: los palpos, los augurios
—siglas inmersas; blastos—. En tus atrios:
las huellas vítreas, las libaciones (glebas fecundas),
los hervideros.

CORAL BRACHO

I hear your body with the quenched and calm intensity
of someone impregnated (of one who
emerges,
who reclines saturated, covered
with sperm) in the coded moisture
(soft, dense oracle: temple)
in the slime, warm reservoirs, deltas,
of her origin; I drink (your exposed, permeable roots;
on your wanton shores
—seething mire—moors) the mossy designs, your
thick sap (mound of drunken vines) I smell
in your deep, vigilant borders, embers,
cascades within your oily jungles. I hear
(your tactile semen) the lodes, larvae (fertile apse) I feel
in your living marshes, your mud: trails,
in your embracing forge: the clues
(I yield
to your anointed thighs, oozing, flowing with light) I hear
within the sour clays, your shores: palpus, omens—signs
submerged—Buds in your atriums:
libations,
fertile clods. Crystalline traces
in the seething springs.

ANA CASTAÑO

Poema

I

      Todo está a punto, señor, izado el llanto
el cortejo de peces y la espuma
el mar temblando.
No habrá ni marineros ni odres ni bitácora
ni hijos ni mujer a bordo;
habrá sólo un manto, el tuyo, cuya misión será la de
      la brisa,
la pavorosa huida
que jamás emprenderán tus hombros ni tus brazos.

II

      El mar convoca a sus pródigas formas con
                      himnos
   erizados
él, tantas veces requerido, se encuentra sin vasallos
busca rabioso a su gigante blanco, recuerda y vocifera.

III

      No hay banderas que basten para esta empresa
   de espanto;
ni una sola sábana de lino en tu navío para nuestros
   cuerpos blandos.

ANA CASTAÑO

Poem

I

The raised cry, all is ready, sir
the courting of fish and foam
the trembling sea.
I will have no sailors, wineskins or binnacle
no sons nor a woman on board;
I bring only a cloak (yours) whose mission will be like
        the breeze,
the terrifying flight
that your shoulders and arms will never understand.

II

The sea assembles its bountiful forms with
                                stinging
     hymns
summoned so often, he stands without vassals
madly he pursues the white giant, remembers and screams.

III

No flags would be adequate for this frightening
     venture;
not a single sheet of linen on your ship for our
     feeble bodies.

IV

      Eres hermoso con el manto en estampida;
y no es la sal lo que blanquea tu barba y la cincela
      como en piedra.
Estás, ah, erquido ante el timón
y es ilegible el vuelo de este azul que te circunda y
      nos aleja.

V

      Como la espuma, pero mucho más inexistente,
soy estrellada contra el mástil; me disuelvo.

VI

      Sólo tú a bordo
no hay en tu navío camarotes ni anclas ni especias
      delicadas
no hay más que tú, señor, sobre este mar virtual
cuyos blasones nunca ostentarán la flor de lis o el
      cardo.

VII

      Treinta y dos días y todo a punto:
nuestra forma de mirarte inacabable
nuestro alambicado llanto
nuestra altura.

IV

      You are handsome with the cloak in frenzied flight;
and it is not salt that whitens your beard and sculpts it
      like a stone.
There you are, erect before the helm
and the soaring blue that surrounds you and separates us
      is unintelligible.

V

      Like the foam but even more ephemeral,
I am shattered against the mast; I dissolve.

VI

      Only you on board
no cabins or anchors or delicate species
      on your ship
only you, sir, on this virtual sea
whose heraldry will never display the fleur-de-lis
      or thistle.

VII

      Thirty-two days and all is ready:
our manner of viewing you is endless
our subtle lament
our lofty place.

VIII

Día treinta y tres: el mar tendido, el aire
desbocado.
Has vencido, señor, ahora sabemos que no hay mar
capaz de resistir el peso de tu barco.

(Yo, que tuve frío, emplazo al timón, único
resto del naufragio, a la doble muerte de su redondez

y de mis letras
norte   sur   este   oeste
para clavar de una vez, como cualquier insecto, en el
impasible mar de todos los mapas, la rosa de los
vientos.)

VIII

Day thirty-three: the extended sea, the uncontrollable
    air.
You have overcome, sir, now we know there is no sea
able to resist the burden of your ship.

      (I, who was cold, locate the helm, the only
remains of the shipwreck, the double death of your
                     roundness
and my letters
      north   south   east   west
to impale at once, like some insect, on the
impassive sea of all the maps, the rose of the
winds.)

TATIANA ESPINASA

Poema

Mañana de quietos horizontes
junto al vacio estanque
de mi miedo:
hay un dolor oculto en tu mirada;
donde mi mano toca
nada encuentro
y es la soledad el fruto de mi juego:
amar lo que no ha sido,
temer lo que no llega.

Y si hoy digo sí a la vida,
mañana un horizonte destruirá la casa...
Y si hoy digo que no,
no habrá ni casa ni horizonte,
ni luz.

Sólo silencio
y este indescifrable amor que siento
por lo que nunca fue,
por lo que siempre ha sido.

Hay amor.
Esta fragancia incontenible que nos daña
(donde nuestra soledad es una,
donde todo parece perpetuarse)
Y no digo sí
ni no;

TATIANA ESPINASA

Poem

Morning of motionless horizons
linked to the empty pool
of my fear:
there is a hidden pain in your gaze;
where my hand touches
I find nothing
and solitude is the fruit of my game:
loving what has not been,
fearing what does not arrive.

And if today I say yes to life,
tomorrow an horizon will destroy my house...
And if today I say no,
I will have no house, horizon,
or light.

Only silence
and this indecipherable love that I feel
for what never was,
for what always has been.

There is love,
this irrepressible fragrance that stains us
(where our solitude is one,
where everything seems to endure)
And I don't say yes
or no;

Yo soy la que espera
tu horizonte,
como una prisionera,
más allá de cuanto fuimos,
más allá de cuanto somos.

Mañana de quietos horizontes
junto al vacio estanque
de mi juego...
Esperando tu amor, tu olvido, tu silencio,
esperando tu amor.
Ahí,
donde nace mi miedo.

I am the one who awaits
your horizon,
like a prisoner,
beyond all that we were,
beyond all that we are.

Morning of motionless horizons
linked to the empty pool
of my game...
Waiting for your love, your neglect, your silence,
waiting for your love.
There,
where my fear is born.

MARINA FE

Duelo

Todo de negro oscuro tu pantano
no consigue tragarme.
Me he vuelto ahora más pesada que el agua,
más ligera que tus espesos lodos.

Aunque quisiera sumergirme,
si quisiera,
no podría penetrarte,
dejarme rodear completamente
por tu aliento de lirio,
por tus brazos de arena,
ni ahogarme en ti
que empiezas a secarte con el tiempo.

MARINA FE

Duel

All the vague blackness of your swamp
could not swallow me.
Now I have become heavier than water
lighter than your clinging mud.

Though I attempt to drown myself,
if I wanted,
I could not penetrate you,
failing to surround me completely
with your lily breath,
your arms of sand,
not smothering myself in you,
because you begin to dry with time.

MARINA FE

Tiempo

mi lamento sin eco en el origen
filtrándose se pierde
sopla en el caracol que lo contiene
y no es voz
ni lamento
ahora

y ahora
desenreda su viento
en la marea de arena
de reloj
invadiendo el espacio donde está
la memoria detenida

MARINA FE

Time

without echo in the source my lament
is lost refining itself
it blows in the shell that contains it
now
neither voice
nor lament

and now
its wind unravels
in the tide of sand
of the clock
invading the space where
memory is confined

KYRA GALVAN

Mis Defectos Entre Las Flores Del Durazno

Las libertades no se dan,
se toman

Kropotkin

Han explotado soles y arcángeles angustiosos.
Blancos que se expanden a violetas.
Playas de lagos de peces extinguidos.
Noches de ingles y palabras dormilonas.
Aventuras camineras y desconocidas.
Sabores de pulque y carne cruda.
Temblores y sacudidas imprevistas.
Movimientos telúricos en los cerebros
consumidos por el oscurantismo circundante.

Un desfloramiento de mí hacia la vida.
Una grieta hacia el cielo andino.
Una mujer aplastada por el tiempo.
Una viscosidad hacia el agua salada.
Una carne viva ante la muerte.
 Y una boca abierta ante la vida.

Te diré: soy mujer cedro mujer angustia
 mujer como trigal como violeta
 como sandía y tormenta.
Busco una isla para gestar en ella,
para inventarme mi libertad y mi cuerpo
 y todos mis movimientos.
Busco mi cara entre las multitudes, mi olor,
en las axilas de mi amante,
mis golondrinas en los cuartos menguantes de la luna.
Mis defectos, entre las flores del durazno.

KYRA GALVAN

My Flaws Among the Peach Blossoms

Freedoms are not given,
they are taken

Kropotkin

Suns and tormented archangels have been exploited.
Whites swelling into violets.
Beaches on lakes of extinct fish.
Nights of groins and dormant words.
Unknown adventures on the road.
Tastes of pulque and raw meat.
Unforeseen tremblings and shocks.
Telluric movements in the brains
consumed by surrounding obscurantism.

A deflowering of me towards life.
A crevice toward the Andean sky.
A woman crushed by time.
A viscosity toward salt water.
Living flesh in the presence of death.
    An open mouth in the presence of life.

I will tell you: I am cedar woman agony woman
    woman like a wheatfield like a violet
    like a watermelon and storm.
I seek an island for gestation,
to fashion my liberty and my body and all my
movements.
I seek my face in the crowds, my odor,
in my lover's armpits,
my swallows in the final quarters of the moon.
My flaws, among the peach blossoms.

Hemos estado sondeando nuestras profundidades
nuestros cuartos oscuros, calculando
el brillo de nuestros caracoles estrella
y nuestros escrupulosos sapos.
Simplemente acariciando nuestros olores
y nuestras accidentales pieles.
No logro saber tu identidad, mi enigma.
Animal luminoso y multifacético
　　que has sublevado mis hordas:
estoy en pie de guerra contra la enajenación.
Estoy en guerra con esa soledad.
　　Me desnudo
mostrando el Gran Miedo de no llegar
a la toma de la libertad.
Y grito mi desamparo fuerte, mi pena.
Te abrazo para oír tu vida y la mía.
Es un buen comienzo.

We have been probing our depths
our darkened rooms, calculating
the radiance of our snail star
and our virtuous toads.
Simply caressing our odors
and our accidental skins.
I still don't know your identity my mystery.
Luminous and intricate animal
    that has aroused my hordes:
I have declared war against alienation.
I am at war with that solitude.
    I disrobe
exposing the Great Fear of not seizing
freedom.
And I scream my durable abandonment, my sorrow.
I embrace you to hear your life and mine.
A good beginning.

KRYA GALVAN

La Revolución Silenciosa

Estoy tocando la flauta
   de mi propia muerte
repasando cada acorde de mis miedos
   sobando mi asfixia
sin querer pensar sentir
   que el abandono ha pasado
   rozando mi nariz
porque es un abismo donde pueden
   suicidarse mis hormonas.
En mi garganta se instalan la falta de voz
   de diálogo/
todos los yaquis desterrados de Sonora
   con sus ojos enormes y sus gargantas secas
con su silencio que recorre sesenta años y premanece.
Todos los minutos que estuvimos tú y yo
   cuerpo a cuerpo
sin pronunciar palabra ni tocarnos/
esos mil días que ahora/se los tragó la tierra
todos los momentos de silencio
que recaen sobre las masas
se agolpan ahí, en mi garganta,
haciendo un nudo
donde confluyen todos
y cada uno de los miedos.
Toco la flauta/convocándome a resistir.

KYRA GALVAN

Silent Revolution

I am playing the flute
    of my own death
reviewing every chord of my fears
    fingering my suffocation
not wanting to think to feel
    that rejection has passed
    touching my nose
because it is an abyss where
    my hormones can commit suicide.
In my throat resides the absence of voice
    of dialogue/
all of the Yaquis exiled from Sonora
    with their enormous eyes and dry throats
with their silence of seventy years that endures.
All those moments you and I were
    body to body
not speaking or touching/
those thousand days that now/swallowed by the earth
all the moments of silence
that collapse on the masses
assemble there, in my throat,
forming a knot
where all the fears converge.
I play the flute/arousing myself to resist.

KYRA GALVAN

Contradicciones Ideológicas Al Lavar Un Plato

Contradicciones ideológicas al lavar un plato, ¿No?
Y también quisiera explicar
por qué me maquillo y por qué uso perfume.
Por qué quiero cantar la belleza del cuerpo masculino.
Quiero aclararme bien ese racismo que existe
entre los hombres y las mujeres.
Aclararme por qué cuando lavo un plato
o coso un botón
él no ha de estar haciendo lo mismo.
Me pinto el ojo
no por automatismo imbécil
sino porque es el único instante en el día

en que regreso a tiempos ajenos y

mi mano se vuelve egipcia y

el rasgo del ojo, se me queda en la Historia.

La sombra en el párpado me embalsama eternamente
como mujer.
Es el rito ancestral del payaso:
mejillas rojas y boca de color.
Me pinto porque así me dignifico como bufón.
Estoy repitiendo/ continuando un acto primitivo.
Es como pintar búfalos en la roca.
Y ya no hay cuevas ni búfalos
pero tengo un cuerpo para texturizarlo a mi gusto.
Uso perfume no porque lo anuncie
Catherine Deneuve o lo use la Bardot
sino porque padezco la enfermedad
del siglo xx, la compulsión de la posesión:
creer que en una botella puede reposar
toda la magia del cosmos,

KYRA GALVAN

Ideological Contradictions On Washing a Plate

Ideological contradictions on washing a plate, right?
Also I would like to explain
why I use make-up and perfume
and why I like to sing the beauty of the masculine body.
I want to clarify properly the racism that exists
between men and women.
To clarify why when I wash a plate
or sew a button
he is not required to do the same.
I put on eye make-up
not as a stupid automatism
but because it is the only moment in the day

when I return to the times of other poeple and

my hand changes to an Egyptian hand and

the dash on the eye remains in History.

The eyeshadow embalms me forever
as woman.
The ancestral rite of the clown:
red cheeks and a colored mouth.
I use make-up because in this way I dignify myself as buffoon.
I am repeating/ continuing a primitive act.
Like painting buffalo on a rock.
Now there are no caves or buffalo
but I have a body I can compose to my taste.
I use perfume not because Catherine Deneuve
advertises it or Bardot uses it
but because I suffer the sickness
of the 20th century, the compulsion of possession:
believing that all the magic of the cosmos
  resides in a bottle,

que me voy a quitar de encima
el olor de la herencia
la gravedad de la crisis capitalista,
porque a pesar de todo/ hembra.
Se dice que las mujeres débiles/ que los hombres
    fuertes.

Sí y nuestras razas tan distintas.

Nuestros sexos tan diversamente complementarios.

Ying & Yang.

La otra parte es el misterio que nunca desnudaremos.
Nunca podré saber —y lo quisiera—
qué se siente estar enfundada en un cuerpo masculino
y ellos no sabrán lo que es olerse a mujer
tener cólicos y jaquecas y
todas esas prendas que solemos usar.
2Dos universos físicos en dialéctica constante
con la nostalgia de una unión duradera
donde la fusión de los dos desconocidos
llegue a la profundidad del entendimiento.
Hay una necesidad compulsiva

a dar razones para la escisión

para agudizar racismos con sonrisas

Y las amigas   y los amigos

            ellos comprenderán
Ellos entienden la distancia que te separa
del amigo / amado / enemigo / desconocido.
    que la reconciliación es un esfuerzo máximo.
La unión, la sublimación
            de nuestros propios misterios.
Que el lavar un plato

significa a veces afirmar

las contradicciones de clase

        entre el hombre y la mujer.

that I will remove from myself
the stench of inheritance
the pressing capitalistic crisis,
because in spite of it all/ female.
One hears that women are weak/ the men
    strong.

Yes and our races so distinct.

Our sexes so diversely complementary.

Ying & Yang.

The other part is the mystery we can never expose.
I will never be able to know —and I would like to—
how it feels to be sheathed in a masculine body
and they will never know what it's like to smell like a woman
to have cramps and migraines and
all those natural gifts we have grown accustomed to.
2Two physical universes in constant dialectic
with nostalgia for a lasting union
where the fusion of two unknowns
might attain a depth of understanding.
There is a compulsive necessity

to give reasons for the division

which only aggravates racism with smiles

the girlfriends   and the boyfriends

        they will understand
They perceive the distance that separates you
from a friend / lover / enemy / stranger.
    that reconciliation is a supreme effort.
Union, the sublimation
    of our own mysteries.
So that washing a plate

sometimes means affirming

the contradictions of class

    between man and woman.

LAURA GONZALEZ DURAN

Te escribo desde los paisajes
que todavía no conozco,
desde las tardes que recuerdo
sin haber estado en ellas.
Te escribo desde la noche,
desde la oscuridad que invade
misteriosamente los rincones
de la pequeña casa
que todavía no habito.
Te escribo desde este cuarto
vacío y blanco
que espera la conquista
de los muebles y de los cuadros,
del verde transcurrir de las plantas
y del aroma mezclado del café
y de la fruta fresca.
Te escribo de lo que no tengo
todavía,
de la frágil seguridad que me viste,
de las decisiones que se confunden
con el color triste de mi pelo.
Te escribo de estas manos solas
que comparten la confusión y el miedo
de unas líneas silenciosas,
de las notas y de los puntillos
que ya no me forman,
de la madera que une sus huecos
a mis dedos para crear una nueva melodía.
Te escribo porque te recuerdo y te veo
aunque no existas,
porque conozco desde hace siglos
el sonido de tus pasos
y te miro sentado frente a la mesa
en la que nunca estuviste.
Te escribo, porque al buscar mi reflejo
en el cristal de la casa
que todavía habito,
me encontré con tu recuerdo claro
en los sueños y en las cosas
con las que todavía vivo.

LAURA GONZALEZ DURAN

I write you from the landscapes
still unknown to me,
from evenings I recall
although I was never there.
I write you from the night,
from the darkness that
mysteriously invades the corners
of the tiny house
where I still do not live.
I write you from this
white and empty room
that awaits the conquest
of furniture and frames,
of the green aging of the plants
and the mixed aroma of coffee
and fresh fruit.
I write you about what I still don't
possess,
the fragile security that clothes me,
about decisions that are confused
with the sad color of my hair.
I write you about these solitary hands
that share confusion and fear
of a few silent lines,
about the notes and social codes
that no longer shape me,
about the wood that joins its hollows
to my fingers and creates a new melody.
I write you because I recall you and see you
although you do not exist,
because for centuries I have known
the sound of your footsteps
and I observe you seated at the table
where you never were.
I write you, because in seeking my reflection
in the window of the house
where I still reside,
I met your vivid memory
in the dreams and the things
still living with me.

LAURA GONZALEZ DURAN

Figura clara y frágil
que recorre las calles de mi cuerpo,
el vacío inmóvil
que habita la palma
de mi mano.
Paisaje de madera
perdido en la raíz
de su corteza
y de su aroma,
en una fuga
de palabras
que no pudieron
dibujar
mi nombre.

LAURA GONZALEZ DURAN

Clear and fragile figure
that roams the streets of my body,
the motionless emptiness
that settles in the palm
of my hand.
Wooden landscape
lost in the root
of its bark
and aroma,
in a flight
of words
unable
to sketch
my name.

LAURA GONZALEZ DURAN

Poema

Porque me reflejo
en pausas
y en silencios
que no conducen
a ninguna
parte,
porque soy viento
que apenas
deja huella,
porque soy tarde
y vivo
del paisaje
cotidiano,
porque soy
de tierra firme
sin raíces,
porque soy
de luz
y de tiempo,
porque soy
de sombra,
porque no encuentro
la blancura
de las horas.

LAURA GONZALEZ DURAN

Poem

Because I reflect
in pauses
and silences
that lead
nowhere,
because I am wind
that barely leaves
a trace,
because I am evening
and alive
in the daily
landscape,
because I am
of the solid earth
without roots,
because I am
of light
and time,
because I am
of shadow,
because I do not engage
the whiteness
of the hours.

ETHEL KRAUZE

Poema

I

El rumor de tus cabellos
                    —fría fronda
navega oscuramente.
Como rumbo de saeta
                    quiebra
                    el tenue perfil,
al oriente viaja
                    traza el último giro
desaparece.

II

Como la rueda de la luna
tus cabellos
giran,
brillan,
se peinan sobre el agua tibia
que hemos dejado aquí
con nuestras furias.
Duerme.
Que el sol navegue ahora
sobre tu rostro.

ETHEL KRAUZE

Poem

I

The whisper of your hair
          —cool foliage
sails obscurely.
Like the course of an arrow
          the delicate profile
          twists
travels to the east
          traces the final turn
vanishes.

II

Like the moon's halo
your hair
spins,
shines,
arranges itself above the tepid water
that we have left behind
with our anger.
Sleep.
So the sun might sail at once
above your face.

MARA LARROSA

Espaldas Negras

a Roberto Bolaño

He visto tu cuerpo mujer, hombre, en la ciudad
He estado solamente viéndote los ojos humanos
He estado junto a tantas mujeres que tienen los
    labios pintados
En la Tierra nacemos con la piel limpiecita y hay
    tantas mujeres que siguen usando sus pañoletas
    desde la adolescencia, la sal les sale de los sobacos
    y los dedos.
Después de haber comido el musgo de las grandes
    paredes, de chillar en los baños de la primaria, de
    besar el pene de Juan Pablo a los 10 años, tengo
    miedo de mover las piernas y los brazos. Ni mi
    voz ni mi cuerpo han desordenado el espacio y así
    creemos florecer sobre el invierno urbano.
Es la luz lo que tiene que entrar en la oscuridad, por
    eso me han crecido los árboles en las orejas, por eso
    se ha extendido mi esencia femenina hasta ti, tan
    cercano tu sexo, tu vientre plano, hermoso. Hasta
    ti temblando, para ti derramando: me he dado
    cuenta que somos semejantes. Amo tus piernas
    blancas, tus brazos blancos.
Por otros es por quien amo, *para los otros.*
Soy feliz por oler a tanta gente.
Ahora, en Ecuador, el agua se llena de zarzas; ahora,
    mientras se desarrollan nuestros ojos y F pide que
    le sirvan con vaso de vidrio en los cafés, he sentido
    TODO lo que nos falta para ser humanos precisos.
F adolescente parte a una mina de sal: le crecerán
    los brazos, y a otros muchachos también les
    crecerán despachando farmacias, fabricando las
    telas, los zapatos, y todos son como el agua que
    está oculta en la Tierra, y todos somos los que
    hacemos el ruido en las banquetas, en las camas.
Amo a F porque está hecho de agua y de hombres.

MARA LARROSA

Ebony Backs

to Roberto Bolaño

I have seen your body woman, man, in the city
I have only been seeing your human eyes
I have been close to so many women with
    painted lips
We are born on this Earth with immaculate skin and there are
    so many women who have worn their muslin bodice
    since adolescence, the salt escapes from the armpits
    and fingers.
After eating moss from the great
    walls, screaming in the primary school baths,
    kissing the penis of Juan Pablo at ten years of age, I
    am afraid to move my arms and legs. Not my voice
    or my body has disordered the space and thus
    we hope to flourish above the urban winter.
The light must penetrate the darkness, that is why
    trees have grown in my ears, why
    I have opened my feminine essence to you, so
    near your sex, your smooth, appealing stomach. Toward
    you trembling, for you overflowing: I have realized
    we are similar. I love your white
    legs, your white arms.
Through others is through whom I love, *for others.*
I am happy to smell so many people.
Now, in Ecuador, the water is filled with brambles; now,
    while our eyes unfold and F asks to be
    served with a glass cup in the cafes, I have sensed
    EVERYTHING we lack to be distinctly human.
F adolescent leaves for a salt mine: his arms will grow,
    and other boys will grow also tending pharmacies,
manufacturing
    fabrics, shoes, and all are similar to the water that
    is hidden in the Earth, we are all those who
    make noise on the sidewalks, in the beds.
I love F because he is made of water and of men.

Gauguin: ¿a dónde vamos? ¿ganaremos la forma
humana? ¿qué es esta larga germinación que se
mueve desde antes que tú conocieras las espaldas
negras con el pelo lacio? ¿esto que se mueve es
acaso el amor largo para que nunca más haya
Charlots en las ciudades?

Gauguin: where are we going? will we achieve the human
   form? what is this lengthy germination that stirred
   before you knew the ebony backs
   with the straight hair? what stirs is perhaps the lingering love
   so that there may be no more
   Charlots in the cities.

VERA LARROSA

Boca Azul

Los dos hombres que amo son viciosos
pero adorables
les he mandado flores a su camarote
y versos bellos y versos malos,
parece que yo fuera el caballero en vez de la dama/
Uno toca el piano
saliendo algodones de sus dedos
como un frankestein risueño y peludo canta una
    balada/
El otro ha cruzado muchos puentes sin vibrar
    siquiera/
y me ha prometido su lengua de buen príncipe/
Mi boca azul grita en los músculos
no hay mejor loción que ésta:
el vaho,
la mujer/
Amo al joven y al viejo sin voltear a ver collares
    escarlata,
ya he lucido los adornos en el palco y flotando entre
    carcajadas
donde mis amigas/ dicen que a los cuarenta se harán
    cirugía plástica/
Talqueada estoy por los vientos/
    la repisa/
también las figuritas de shadró han sido votadas de
—ay, esos vientos/—
talqueada voy al espejo a sorprender a mis mejillas,
más que rubor/
más polen/
¿Cuándo seré amada en los hoteles y en los campos?
¿Cuándo peinaré la melena larga a corta de mis
    señores?

VERA LARROSA

Blue Mouth

The two men I love are vicious
but adorable
I have sent flowers to their cabin
as well as good and bad verses,
it seems that I play the gentleman instead of the lady/
One plays the piano
issuing cotton from his fingers
like a smiling, hairy Frankenstein he sings a
    ballad/
The other has crossed many bridges without
    shaking/
and has offered me his language of a good prince/
My blue mouth screams in the muscles
no better cleansing than this:
the steam,
woman/
I love the young and old men without rolling over to see scarlet
    necklaces,
and I have displayed the adornments at the theater and floating
    between bursts of laughter
where my friends/ they say that by forty they will have
    plastic surgery/
I am powdered by the winds/
    the ledge/
also the tiny shadro figures have been approved by
—oh, these winds/—
powdered I approach the mirror to surprise my cheeks,
more than blush/
more pollen/
When will I be loved in hotels and fields?
When will I comb the long or short hair of my
    men?

El frasco de pastillas suicidas
viajará en mi carne/
Habrá un drama hasta en mis calcetines si el impacto
　y el éter florecen/
Ya no resisto los abandonos,
la culpa ha empezado a soltar un resplandor de oros
　y zafiros
Los dos hombres que amo son viciosos
pero unos encantos
pero unos elefantes.
Para ellos soy un diminuto grano de pimienta/
El frasco,
las migajas empiezan a caminar en el tocador/
Mis amores abren sus piernas lanzándose al terror
el terror de una putanga en minifalda/
El frasco de pastillas está bailando/
tomo una tomo dos de esas migajas azules
hasta nunca culo flácido
nada supiste de dóciles vestidos/
Hasta nunca horizonte de machos/

Will the small bottle of suicidal tablets
travel in my flesh?
There will be a drama down to my socks if the impact
    and the ether flourish/
I can no longer endure the rejections,
reproach has begun to release a flashing of golds
    and sapphires
The two men I love are vicious
but some enchanting
others elephants
To them I am a tiny grain of pepper/
The small bottle,
the grains begin to stir on the dressing table/
My lovers spread their legs throwing themselves at terror
the terror of a cheap whore in miniskirt/
The small bottle of pills is dancing/
I take one then a second of these blue grains
farewell forever flabby ass
you knew nothing about docile clothes/
farewell forever horizon of males/

SOCORRO LEON FEMAT

La noche es un segundo
sumergido en la luz
es un pedazo de plomo
que rueda por debajo
de los ejes del día
es un motivo para oír
con más claridad el zumbido
de los aparatos eléctricos
que acompasan nuestros sueños
enjaulados en el olvido
como palomas que alguna vez
escapan para ascender la madrugada
dejando sus plumas sus huellas
de mediaestrella en la superficie
esférica de la conciencia.

SOCORRO LEON FEMAT

Night is an instant
submerged in light
a piece of lead
rolling beneath
the axis of day
it is a reason for hearing
the distinct humming
of electric appliances
that direct our dreams
caged in oblivion
like doves that occasionally
escape to promote the dawn
leaving their feathers, their half-star
tracks on the spherical
surface of the conscience.

SOCORRO LEON FEMAT

Pero la puerta que da al vacío
está abierto día y noche
y el vacío está saturado de objetos
de voces de motores de ruido de espera
trás de una ventanilla de transistores
de luces de aparadores de calles
interminables como lenguas
que se precipitan en la pendiente
de una sóla garganta de mañanas
que sudan un rocío tiznado y amargo
de horas que van río abajo
como peces muertos de las miles
de ratas que habitan con su irremediable
y eterna ceguera el alcantarillado
llenando de sus ruidos las noches
y el silencio extraño de las calles despobladas
De una soledad aberrante que nos extravía
andamos angustiados como presas
buscándonos en cada compartimiento
de la casa en la ciudad en un rostro
que se nos parece.

SOCORRO LEON FEMAT

But the door that faces the void
is open day and night
and the void is brimming with objects
with voices motors noises and waiting
behind a small window of transistors
lights appliances and interminable
streets like tongues
that fall on the slope
of a single throat of tomorrows
that perspire a sooty bitter dew
of hours moving down river
like dead fish by the thousands
of rats that live with their incurable
eternal blindness in the sewer
overflowing the nights with their noise
and the strange silence of the deserted streets.
With an abnormal loneliness that leads us astray
we walk like tormented prey
searching in every section
of the house in the city in a face
that resembles ourselves.

SOCORRO LEON FEMAT

Poema

Pesado cargar de pensamientos
al tiempo de las notas
de cada paso.

Son los años del conflicto
y los días contradictorios
es el tiempo en que se piensa.

La locura muerde con sus finos dientes
cada centímetro de la cabeza
hasta que los ojos ven lúcidamente
los huesos del mundo.

Se abaten   los tradicionales sentimientos.

Y entonces te flagelan
los que no tienen problemas
y tejen sueños de grandeza
los amorosos beatos
las agusanadas vírgenes
que bordan el ajuar de sal.

Los buenos que invierten
el significado de las palabras
y pasan la vida como un manantial.

Todos en recua se van al cielo
sin pensamiento   conflicto
contradicción y locura.

SOCORRO LEON FEMAT

Poem

Heavy burden of thoughts
at the time of notes
and every step.

They are the conflict years
and the contradictory days
a time when one reflects.

Madness bites each centimeter of the head
with its sharpened teeth
until the eyes clearly see
the bones of the world.

Traditional sentiments   subside.

Then those without problems
whip you
and weave dreams of greatness
the loving and the blessed
the wormy virgins
who embroider a trousseau of salt.

The good people reverse
the meaning of words
and let life go by like a flowing spring.

All of them go to heaven in a band
without thought   conflict
contradiction or madness.

PURA LOPEZ COLOME

Castres

Humo
sombra de la luz que escapa
(se queda quieto en el barandal
huele a manzana)

no pasa nada
si la gente entra o sale del hotel
pelando una fruta   revuelto el pelo
tal vez pensando en algo
o con un nudo en la garganta
nada en absoluto

los pájaros casi se estrellan
en los rostros sobre las fachadas
están ahí
seguramente dormirán dentro de un rato
cuando esta claridad de las once de la noche acabe
porque es verano

(real es que no haya nada
que nada llegue a suceder deveras
que aun desde la terraza
el origen del lugar no exista)

PURA LOPEZ COLOME

Castres

Smoke
shadow of light that flees
(remains motionless on the railing
smells like apple)

nothing happens
if people enter or leave the hotel
peeling a piece of fruit   hair a mess
perhaps thinking about something
or with a lump in the throat
absolutely nothing

the birds nearly crash
into the faces above the facades
they are there
surely they will sleep in a little while
when this brightness of eleven o'clock on a summer's night
fades away

(the truth is there is nothing
that nothing truly occurs
that not even from the balcony
does the source of the place exist)

BLANCA LUZ PULIDO

Del Fuego

Toda la noche vi crecer el fuego.
José Emilio Pacheco

Toda la noche vi crecer el fuego
y no pude tocarlo
ni sumarme a su encuentro luminoso.

Toda la noche supe de su danza
de su comercio con el viento
y no quise unirme a su llegada
ni celebrar su magnífico retorno.

El fuego es la renuncia de las cosas
a su aspecto tenaz, a su dibujo.

Toda la noche vi crecer el fuego
y no conocí su voz
ni apuré su llama

y aquí estoy

en este paisaje de cenizas.

BLANCA LUZ PULIDO

From the Fire

All night I saw the fire growing.
José Emilio Pacheco

All night I saw the fire growing
and I could not touch it
or join in its radiant motion.

All night I was aware of its dance
of its dealings with the wind
refusing to embrace its arrival
or celebrate its splendid return.

Fire is the renunciation of the enduring features
of things, of their pattern.

All night I saw the fire growing
its voice was unknown
and I did not stifle the flames

And here I am

in this landscape of ashes.

BLANCA LUZ PULIDO

Presagio

Nada en el mundo te alcanza todavía:
son tus labios de sombra,
y tu voz un fantasma.

Has surgido a la luz de mis dos ojos,
y te aumenta mi sangre,
y te encumbran mis venas.

Ya sin saberlo te acercas a tu forma,
y encenderás la llama
en la incesante noche que te espera.

Y sin saberlo escribirás tu nombre,
tu no nacido nombre, entre mis labios.

BLANCA LUZ PULIDO

Omen

Nothing in the world has overtaken you yet:
your lips are shadow,
your voice a phantom.

You have risen to the light of my two eyes,
my blood enriches you,
and my veins exalt you.

Without knowing it you move closer to your form,
and you will kindle the flame
in the endless night that awaits you.

Without knowing it you will write your name,
your unborn name, between my lips.

BLANCA LUZ PULIDO

Noche

La noche inmemorial, pródiga noche
de los pactos oscuros, innombrables,
de las siniestras, ocultas voluntades
que a la mención del día empalidecen;
la noche feraz, la noche cómplice
que despliega su sombra como un manto
sigiloso y ambiguo; torva noche
agazapada en las márgenes del día
anticipando su reino silencioso;
pero la noche débil, sola espera,
aire que corre en el país de nadie,
tierra del eco, junta de fantasmas:
cántaro negro que en la luz se rompe.

BLANCA LUZ PULIDO

Night

Immemorial night, lavish night
of dark, unmentionable pacts,
of sinister, hidden wishes
that grow pale at the mention of day;
the fertile night, accomplice night
that unfurls its shadow like a shrouded
ambiguous blanket; fierce night
crouched on the boundaries of day
awaiting its silent kingdom;
but the feeble night waits alone,
a wind that blows in no one's country,
land of the echo, gathering place of ghosts:
black vessel that shatters in the light.

GABRIELA RABAGO PALAFOX

Haikús

4

La madrugada.
Los pájaros enlazan
sus cantos rotos.

97

Presiente el ave
que la ama el toro.
Escalofrío.

105

Patios llovidos.
El ruido de tus pasos
huele a marisma.

163

Viento de marzo,
¿por qué silbas amores
a la estatua?

GABRIELA RABAGO PALAFOX

Haikus

4

Daybreak.
The birds harmonize
their scattered songs.

97

The bird senses
the love of the bull.
A shiver of fear.

105

Rainy courtyards.
The sound of your steps
smells like a marsh.

163

March wind,
why do you whistle of love
to the statue?

PERLA SCHWARTZ

Amor Y Geometría

Amor geométrico.
Nuestras vidas siempre han sido paralelas,
hoy faltan a su ley
al unirse:
formar un ángulo menor de un grado,
lentamente acercarse
del obtuso al recto
hasta conformar el más pequeño agudo
que existe y que amenaza
en convertirse en una línea;
menor distancia intermedia,
nuestra pasión nace de dos;
corazón aritmético que tiene
la base firme de un trapecio.

PERLA SCHWARTZ

Love and Geometry

Geometric love.
Our lives have always been parallel,
today they break the rule
by merging;
forming an angle less than one degree,
slowly approaching
from the obtuse to the straight
adjusting to the smallest acute angle
that exists and which threatens
to transform itself into a line;
less intervening distance,
our passion is born of two;
arithmetical heart with
a solid trapeze base.

PERLA SCHWARTZ

El Trazo De La Memoria

Los recuerdos se van ausentando,
se vuelven fantasmas,
materia transparente casi incolora,
son poco menos que humo sobrevolando la habitación,
cigarrillos consumidos en la noche intensa.

La desesperación crece por recuperar recuerdos,
imágenes que se van perdiendo entre el desván
que no alcanza a detener su propia historia,
relato que se desborda conforme el tiempo
invade un territorio de exclusividad.
¿Qué quedó de los años?
¿Qué de las intensas emociones
de esas noches de verano ya perdidas entre framboyanes
y el vino rojo acaso verde corriendo
entre las venas y las palabras?
¿A dónde están esos primeros lances amorosos
del tigre sobre su víctima, quien se defiende
bajo las sábanas, temerosa de una nueva agresión?

Se ha ausentado por siempre la existencialista
vestida de negro
recargada entre las mesas de libros,
quizás devorada por su propia asfixia.
Por siempre está ausente
aquella que toma copas con los amigos en el bar,
aquella que se pierde en la noche del sur
y la madre la espera impaciente.
Tantas vivencias desviadas de su cauce,
tantos momentos que son poco menos que polvo
entre las telarañas de una memoria
que opta por desconocerse,

PERLA SCHWARTZ

The Design of Memory

The memories are receding,
becoming phantoms,
transparent almost colorless matter,
slightly less than smoke hovering in the room,
cigarettes consumed in the depths of night.

Recapturing memories breeds desperation,
images escaping through the loft
that cannot restrain their special story,
a tale that overflows as time
invades the exclusive realm.
What was left of the years?
What about the intense emotions
of those summer nights now lost among the flaming trees
and the red wine perhaps a little green running
between the veins and the words?
What about those first amorous adventures
of the tiger over its victim, who defends herself
beneath the sheets, fearful of renewed attack?

The existentialist has vanished forever
dressed in black
leaning against the book tables
perhaps devoured by her own suffocation.
Gone forever is
the one who drank with her friends in the bar,
the one who wanders in the southern night
and whose mother impatiently awaits.
So many experiences diverted from their course,
so may moments even less than dust
on the cobwebs of a memory
that chooses to be unknown,

memoria que teme descubrirse desnuda
con su piel dorada de aquella primavera
en que bastaba corretear la copa de amareto
y trasladarse,
y estremecerse;
las pieles de los lobos esteparios rescatadas
entre cartas amarillas,
cercanas y lejanas de ese Vallejo
que las unió con un: "se encenderá mi hormiga..."

La memoria que no quiere traicionar
la aparente placidez del presente
de las risas del chiquillo que corretea
entre los muebles de la casa,
el trazo de la memoria que descorre sigilosa su velo
en la tarde de ruidos que se apartan
y es posible acceder al recuerdo venturoso
de los azules coloreados por el rojo del Mediterráneo
imponiéndose a las brasas del cielo,
presidiendo a los infatigables caminantes,
a los insobornables amigos
en esos días tan necesarios de Israel,
donde se convocaron ante las piedras de Césarea,
aquellos que firmaron un pacto de amistad milenaria,
aquellos que con la flauta acercaron la música
de sus complicidades lanzadas
entre los campos de girasoles,
borrando las heridas del amor, de la vida y de la muerte.
Pero los recuerdos se desgastan
sin soportar su demasiada realidad.
Sucede que la memoria también se cansa.
Sucede que la memoria opta por sumergirse
en el letargo del silencio.

a memory afraid of finding itself naked
with its skin tanned by that springtime
when it was enough to pursue the glass of Amaretto,
to be in motion,
and tremble,
the skins of steppenwolves recovered
among yellowed letters,
so near and far from the Vallejo
that united them with: "my ant will catch fire..."

Memory does not wish to betray
the apparent calm of the present
or the laughter of a child who runs
around the furniture in the house,
the design of memory that secretly removes its veil
in the evening of noises that withdraw
and it is possible to give in to a happy recollection
of the blues colored by the red of the Mediterranean
imposing itself on the embers of the sky,
presiding over the tireless travelers,
the incorruptible friends
from those days so essential to Israel,
where those who signed the ancient friendship pact
gathered before the rocks of Caeserea,
those who approached the music of their determined schemes
with a flute
in sunflower fields,
erasing the wounds of love, life and of death.
But the memories waste away
unable to support their excessive reality.
It happens that memory also grows weary.
It happens that memory chooses to immerse itself
in the lethargy of silence.

FRIDA VARINIA

Los hombres
intuíamos
    eran necesarios
        pero había pocos
            pocos muñecos

    Teníamos que inventarlos

    Ya no se inventan
        están ahí esperándonos
            esperándonos crecer

    somos sus muñecas
        y las nuestras lloran y crecen
    hablan
        y las otras
            se entierran

FRIDA VARINIA

Men
we sensed
were necessary
but there were few
too few male dolls

We had to invent them

They are no longer invented
they are there waiting for us
waiting for us to mature

we are their dolls
and our dolls cry and grow up
they speak
and the others
are buried

FRIDA VARINIA

Poema

Creo que ya vas a llegar y no eres tú,
me pregunto si alguna parte de vida
será para sentirla contigo.
Ni sé quién eres ni cómo se te llama
mas te añadí en el memorándum nuevo
donde menciono lineas ya de ti.
Escucha si existes
entonces donde habites,
inquieta tu calma y piensa en mí;
y sabe que no te ignoro,
que añoro un pasado sin ti
y espero antes de perderme
en la desesperanza, reconocerte.

FRIDA VARINIA

Poem

I am convinced you will arrive and not be you,
I ask if there will be some part of life
to be explored with you.
But I don't know who you are or what your name is
only what I added to you in the new notebook
where I refer to lines already about you.
Listen if you exist
then where you live,
disturb your calm and think of me;
and realize I am aware of you,
that I long for a past without you
and that I hope before losing myself
in despair, to recognize you.

VERONICA VOLKOW

Si Se Viera Amanecer...

si se viera amanecer
a la estrella secreta del deseo
a esa aurora inminente
germinada siempre en la destrucción de su fuego
si crecieran las ramas sangrientas de las manos
y la sepulta atlántida del ojo resurgiera
bajo un sol de sueño
si todos los gestos suspensos tuvieran un pleno
  florecimiento
y desencadenaran la savia
de las simientes prohibidas
y el árbol infinito de todos los conocimientos
si se rompieran los párpados
cristalinos del agua
y la semilla enterrada en su tierra de azogue
o la memoria que encauza
el rostro en sus reflejos
esa memoria que corta
el avance del mar con un espejo
¡ay! para siempre idéntico
si se rompiera
si se rompiera
y amaneciera la estrella secreta del deseo

VERONICA VOLKOW

If the Dawning of a Hidden Star...

If the dawning of a hidden star
of desire could be seen
that impending daybreak
always nourished in its smothered fire
if the bloody branches of the hands could grow
and the buried atlantis of the eye could reappear
beneath a sun of dream
if all the dangling gestures had an abundant
    flowering
and they could release the sap
of forbidden seeds
and the infinite tree of all knowledge
if they could shatter the crystal
eyelids of water
and the seed buried in mercury soil
or the memory that guides
the face in its reflections
that memory which severs
the advancing sea with a mirror
oh! forever identical
if it could shatter
if it could shatter
and the hidden star of desire could be the dawn

ADRIANA YAÑEZ

El miedo es una planta
Crece   por dentro
Echa raices de noche
Canta en la profundidad de la caverna
Son rezos   murmullos   palabras antiguas   rumor terral
(Su aliento próximo te recorre el cuerpo)
Es el silencio que se piensa
Es el alga tiritando
Es la planta de los muertos
    el árbol de las tumbas y de los ecos

ADRIANA YAÑEZ

Fear is a plant
It flourishes   within
extending roots in the night
It chants in the cavern depths
Prayers   whispers   ancient words   land murmur
(Its familiar breath roams the body)
It is the silence that is imagined
The trembling seaweed
Plant of the dead
     the tree of tombs and echoes

ADRIANA YAÑEZ

Inconstantes en mí las presencias del clown
                        aquella noche
De infancia deshabitada
              en un tiempo lejano y ahora incierto
Donde todo era verdad
La mirada agradecía el terror
              de las más alucinantes contorsiones
Cuando los albinos trapecistas
Oscilaban
        de uno al otro lado de la vida
Intercambiando en la repelencia de cada contacto
        enormes bocas
        cavernas de lentejuelas multicolores
Necesariamente pendulares
Las presencias de las niñas que nunca fuí
        de las muchas muñequitas de papel presas
En la realidad oblicua de un rayo de luz
Sobre el telón rojo

ADRIANA YAÑEZ

The changeable presence of the clown in me
                              that night
Deprived of childhood
                 in a distant time and now uncertain
Where all was truth
The gaze thankful for the terror
                 of the most hallucinating contortions
When albino trapeze artists
Swayed
        from one side of life to the other
Exchanging in the repulsion of each connection
                      enormous mouths
                      caverns of multicolor sequins
Unavoidably pendular
Presences of little girls I never was
        of many captive paper dolls
In the oblique reality of a light ray
Above the red curtain

ADRIANA YAÑEZ

Fragmentos huyen
Callan mi arquitectura   a golpes
(acto inconcluso   forma fracasada)
Aristas sonámbulas
Paren ausencias en el quicio de mi corazón
Puntual se cierne la noche
Dolor   curva sin epicentro
Sobre mi espalda perfecta

ADRIANA YAÑEZ

Fragments flee
Stifling my architecture   with blows
(unfinished act   a futile form)
Sleepwalking artists
Create absences in the framework of my heart
The night soars on schedule
Pain curves without epicenter
Above my perfect back.

NOTES ON CONTRIBUTORS

PATRICIA ALVAREZ AVENDAÑO was born in Aguascalientes in 1954. Her poems have appeared in a number of literary jounals including *Tierra Adentro*. Her interests have included the study of artistic tapestry.

LILIA BARBACHANO was born in Mexico City in 1958. In 1981 she published a book of poems, *Las figuras dormidas del destino*. She has published translations of James Joyce and Joseph Brodsky, and is currently working with the Mexican mission at the United Nations.

HILDA BAUTISTA was born in Mexico City in 1956. She has published two volumes of poetry to date, *Pincel de sueños* in 1980 and *A través del cristal* in 1987. A third book, *Poemas*, will appear soon.

SABINA BERMAN was born in Mexico City in 1956. She is a poet and dramatist who has received four Premio Nacional de Teatro awards since 1979. Her poetry volumes include *Poemas del agua* in 1986 and *Lunas* in 1988.

CARMEN BOULLOSA was born in Mexico City in 1954. She is a poet, dramatist, and novelist. Her book of poems, *Ingobernable*, was published in 1979 by UNAM. She has published two novels (*Mejor desaparece* and *Antes*) since 1987.

CORAL BRACHO was born in Mexico City in 1951. Her 1981 poetry volume, *El ser que va a morir*, was awarded the Premio Nacional de Poesía in Mexico. Her collected poems were recently published by Fondo de cultura económica (*Bajo el destello líquido: Poesía 1977-1981*),

ANA CASTAÑO was born in Mexico City in 1956. Her poems have appeared in a number of literary reviews and journals including *El Telar*, *Versus*, *Vida universitaria*, *Cartapacios*, and *Cuadernillos de taller*.

TATIANA ESPINASA was born in Mexico City in 1959. She has published poetry, short fiction, and philosophical essays in various journals including *La casa del tiempo*, *La orquesta*, and *La gaceta*. In 1979 she published a book of short fiction with Artifice ediciones.

MARINA FE was born in Mexico City in 1951. She is a poet, translator (from English, French and Portuguese), and essayist whose work has appeared in numerous journals including *Siempre, Mujeres, Revista de la universidad de México*, and *Thesis*.

KYRA GALVAN was born in Mexico City in 1956. She has published three books of poetry—*Un pequeño moretón en la piel de nadie* (1982), *Un tren de luz* (with two other poets in 1982), and *Alabanza escribo* (1989). She has also published translations from Russian and English. In 1980 she received the National Young Poets award from the Instituto Nacional de Bellas Artes in Mexico.

LAURA GONZALEZ DURAN was born in Mexico City in 1952. Her latest book of poetry titled *La palabra* will appear in 1990. Her translations of contemporary French and Canadian poetry were published recently in *Periódico de poesía*.

ETHEL KRAUZE was born in Mexico City in 1954. Since 1982, she has published ten volumes that include books of poetry and short fiction as well as novels. Her most recent book of poetry, *Ha venido a buscarte*, appeared in 1989.

MARA LARROSA was born in Mexico City in 1956. She has studied painting and published her poetry in *Pájaro de calor, Versus, Correspondencia infra, Pural*, and *Revista mexicana de cultura*.

VERA LARROSA was born in Mexico City in 1957. She has studied dance and theater and published her poetry in *La cultura en México, Revista mexicana de cultura*, and *Versus*.

SOCORRO LEON FEMAT was born in Mexico City in 1955. She has published two books of poetry, *Bajo la arena* (1978) and *De polvo, agonía y tiempo* (1983).

PURA LOPEZ COLOME was born in Mexico City in 1952. Her poetry has appeared in *Boletín de la capilla alfonsina, Punto de partida*, and *Cartapacios*. She has also published translations of poetry by Ginsberg, W.C. Williams, Pound, Eliot, Ferlinghetti, Cummings, and Elizabeth Bishop.

BLANCA LUZ PULIDO was born in Teoloyucán in 1956. Her poems have appeared in several Mexican journals and she has published two books of poems: *Fundaciones* (1979) and *Ensayo de un árbol* (1983).

GABRIELA RABAGO PALAFOX was born in Mexico City in 1950. Her poems have been published in Mexican journals including *El heraldo cultural*.

PERLA SCHWARTZ was born in Mexico City in 1956. She has published seven books—five poetry volumes and two collections of essays. Her recent book, *El quebranto del silencio*, was a selection of essays dealing with twentieth-century women poets who have committed suicide.

FRIDA VARINIA was born in Mexico City in 1960. Her poetry has appeared in many anthologies and journals. In addition, she has edited several anthologies including *Avidas mareas: selección de la poesía joven mexicana* (1988), and *El cuerpo del deseo: antología de poesía erótica feminina* (1989).

VERONICA VOLKOW was born in Mexico City in 1955. She has published four volumes of poetry since 1974. Her latest book of poems. *Los caminos*, was published in 1989. Since 1986, she has published translations of the poetry of Elizabeth Bishop, Michael Hamburger, and John Ashbery.

ADRIANA YAÑEZ was born in Mexico City in 1954. She is a poet, translator (from French and Catalan), and essayist. Her poems have appeared in numerous journals and her book, *El movimiento surrealista*, was published in 1979.